discovermore

Exploring Life Science

Understanding Plant Structures

Ernest Brazzos

Britannica®
Educational Publishing
IN ASSOCIATION WITH
THE ROSEN PUBLISHING GROUP

Published in 2025 by The Rosen Publishing Group, Inc.
2544 Clinton Street, Buffalo, NY 14224

Editor: Brianna Propis
Book Design: Michael Flynn

Photo Credits: Cover LiliGraphie/Shutterstock.com; (series background) Dai Yim/Shutterstock.com; p. 4 (left) IM_photo/Shutterstock.com; p. 4 (right) Sardo Michael/Shutterstock.com; p. 5 Tamiflu/Shutterstock.com; p. 7 malshkoff/Shutterstock.com; p. 8 Sean Pavone/Shutterstock.com; p. 9 nnattalli/Shutterstock.com; p. 11 (top) Tetiana Leman/Shutterstock.com; p. 11 (bottom) TonelloPhotography/Shutterstock.com; p. 12 Neirfy/Shutterstock.com; p. 13 Hannamariah/Shutterstock.com; p. 14 pernsanitfoto/Shutterstock.com; p. 15 Pakapan Chankhao/Shutterstock.com; p. 16 Kazakova Maryia/Shutterstock.com; p. 17 Jack Hong/Shutterstock.com; p. 19 bergamont/Shutterstock.com; p. 20 Vronivis/Shutterstock.com; p. 21 allit/Shutterstock.com; p. 23 (top) New Africa/Shutterstock.com; p. 23 (bottom) GraphicsRF.com/Shutterstock.com; p. 24 Christoph Burgstedt/Shutterstock.com; p. 25 GraphicsRF.com/Shutterstock.com; p. 26 Dubova/Shutterstock.com; p. 27 Job Narinnate/Shutterstock.com; p. 29 Amanda Carden/Shutterstock.com.

Library of Congress Cataloging-in-Publication Data

Names: Brazzos, Ernest, author.
Title: Understanding plant structures / Ernest Brazzos.
Description: Buffalo : Britannica Educational Publishing, [2025] | Series: Discover more! exploring life science | Includes bibliographical references and index.
Identifiers: LCCN 2023051665 (print) | LCCN 2023051666 (ebook) | ISBN 9781641901741 (library binding) | ISBN 9781641901734 (paperback) | ISBN 9781641901758 (ebook)
Subjects: LCSH: Botany--Juvenile literature. | Plant physiology--Juvenile literature. | Plants--Juvenile literature.
Classification: LCC QK49 .B749 2025 (print) | LCC QK49 (ebook) | DDC 580--dc23/eng/20231219
LC record available at https://lccn.loc.gov/2023051665
LC ebook record available at https://lccn.loc.gov/2023051666

Manufactured in the United States of America

CPSIA Compliance Information: Batch #CSBRIT25. For further information contact Rosen Publishing at 1-800-237-9932.

Contents

Plant Life

The tall trees that give us shade, the flowers in our garden, and the grass underneath our feet are all plants, although they look very different from one another. There are plants all over the world. They live in hot, warm, and cold places. Plants grow in dirt, in water, and even on other plants! They're living things—just like us—which means they grow, feed, and reproduce.

REDWOOD TREE

DUCKWEED

Plants can be as large as redwood trees or as small as duckweed, a kind of water plant.

These flowers are called bleeding hearts. Can you tell why they were given this name?

Plants come in a variety of sizes, shapes, and colors, but most of them still have the same parts and functions. Most plants have roots, stems, leaves, flowers, and fruit. Every part of a plant has a particular role to help the plant survive, grow, and reproduce.

Consider This

As you read this book, try to find the similarities and differences between various plants. For example, what do all roots, stems, and flowers have in common? How are they different?

Where Are the Roots?

Most plants' roots grow under the ground, so we can't see them from above. Roots hold plants in the ground. They help stop plants from being blown away by the wind.

Roots are covered in tiny hairs. Water and nutrients from the soil soak into the root hairs and travel up the roots to the rest of the plant through a process called **osmosis**. This is important for a plant's ability to live and grow.

Every type of plant has a different type of root. Some plants have many small roots that grow in different directions. Other plants have one big root called a taproot that is firm and tough. The taproot grows down vertically into the soil.

WORD WISE

OSMOSIS IS THE MOVEMENT OF WATER FROM AN AREA OF HIGHER CONCENTRATION IN A SOLUTE (SUCH AS SUGAR) TO AN AREA OF LOWER CONCENTRATION.

These are the roots of soybean plants.

Stem or Straw?

Stems are plant parts that you can see from above the ground. A stem is the stalk from which buds, shoots, and leaves grow. Stems have hollow tubes inside them. These work like drinking straws. They send water and nutrients upwards from the roots and carry them to other parts of the plant.

Certain bamboo species have stems that can grow around 35 inches (91 cm) in a day!

Plants with thin stems like climbing hydrangea, a type of flower, attach themselves to walls or fences for support.

Like plants themselves, stems can come in a variety of shapes and sizes. Plants can have one stem or many. Some plants' stems have thorns. Many stems are straight and firm. Others are thinner, floppier, and unable to stand upright.

Consider This

Not only do stems move water into a plant, but they help them to stand up. What do you think would happen to a plant if the stem was unable to move water?

Tree Trunks

Tree stems—called trunks—are strong, thick, and tall. Trees have strong stems so they can hold up heavy branches that grow leaves and flowers. Tree trunks are covered in a tough outer layer called bark. Bark is like a protective casing over the tree trunk inside, keeping it safe.

Tree trunks are made of wood, a sturdy plant material. A tree grows by producing new layers of wood around the trunk, just under the bark. Over time, the wood in the middle of the tree dies and becomes hard, making the trunk strong.

Every tree has layers inside. The inner bark sends sap and sugars from a tree's leaves to feed the rest of the tree.

compare and contrast

Based on what you have learned, how are tree trunks similar to smaller plant stems? How are they different?

Trunks contain rings, or circular lines inside of the tree. They can tell you how old the tree is, as well as the weather history at the location where it grew.

Leave It Be

Leaves can be large or small, and they can be all sorts of beautiful colors—but they have important tasks. Leaves make food for plants by a process called photosynthesis. They use **energy** from sunlight to turn water and air into food. Water travels from the roots of a plant to its leaves. Tiny holes in the bottom of the leaves allow air to move through.

Leaves change colors during autumn because chlorophyll production slows down. Chlorophyll is what gives leaves their green color. It's like their food!

These photos show the same tree and its changes during the four seasons.

Stems hold up leaves. They also spread leaves out so they can get as much light as possible. Plants use the food made in leaves to grow and to make other plant parts.

Some trees drop their leaves in fall. Their leaves stop making food and then fall to the ground. The trees grow new leaves in the spring, storing their energy during the winter by having bare branches.

WORD WISE

ENERGY IS THE POWER FROM RESOURCES THAT HELP LIVING THINGS WORK, MOVE, LIVE, AND GROW.

Spiky Leaves

Plants usually have wide, flat leaves to receive more sunlight. Some plants have special leaves that are long and thin. These leaves are called needles or spines.

The spines on cactus plants are a type of leaf. Cactus plants make food in their green stems, not their leaves. Their sharp leaves help to stop animals from eating their stems.

Cactus spines are as hard and strong as wood or bamboo!

Many animals make pine trees their home, such as red woodpeckers.

The types of trees that have needle leaves are called pines and firs. These needles can make food. They are a special shape to help them survive the cold. Needles are not damaged by snow and ice. They stay on the tree through the winter, which is where evergreen trees get their name!

Consider This

Animals such as camels can consume cactuses, and animals such as squirrels can eat pine needles. What similar adaptations must both animals have if they can consume pointy needles in their environments?

Petals and Pollen

Most plants grow flowers. Like leaves, flowers come in many sizes, shapes, and colors. Flowers grow the seeds that many plants later use to reproduce. Most flowers have petals. Inside the petals are male parts called stamens, a female part called a pistil, or both. Stamens hold a powder called pollen. A flower can start to grow seeds—or reproduce—when pollen is moved from a stamen to a pistil.

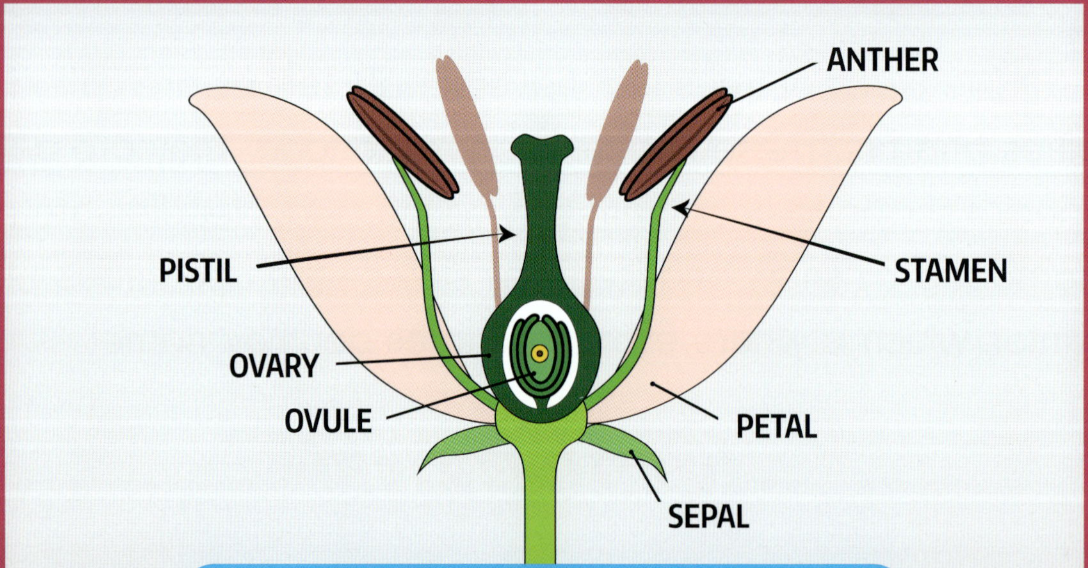

This drawing shows the parts of a flower.

Bees can help by relocating pollen from flower to flower. The pollen sticks to the hair on the bees' legs and comes off on the next flower they land on.

Nectar is a sweet, sugary liquid that some flowers produce. Flowers often have colorful petals that attract insects or small birds. When these animals visit flowers to drink nectar, pollen rubs onto their bodies. When the animals visit a new flower, the pollen rubs onto its pistil. This is called pollination. A flower can begin to grow seeds and reproduce after being pollinated.

Fruits and Nuts

Seeds begin to grow after a flower has been pollinated and the **ovules** are fertilized. Fruits grow around the seeds to protect them. Some fruits, such as oranges, are soft, juicy, and sweet. Other fruits, such as nuts, are hard and dry. Some fruits, such as cherries, contain one seed while others, like melons, have many seeds.

Fruits can move their own seeds! After an animal eats fruit, the seeds come out in its droppings. Squirrels and chipmunks gather nuts and bury them to eat later. Sometimes the animals forget about the nuts, and—when their hard fruit cases rot away—the seeds begin to grow.

Consider This

Fruits are from a plant's flowers and contain seeds, while vegetables are the parts of a plant you can eat—such as the leaves and bulbs. Many people consider tomatoes and cucumbers to be vegetables, but scientifically they are fruit. Why do you think this is?

Kiwi seeds are tiny and black. They form a circle inside the fruit.

WORD WISE

OVULES ARE SMALL STRUCTURES IN THE PLANT THAT GROW INTO FRUIT SEEDS.

Conifer Cones

Some trees and shrubs grow cones instead of flowers and fruit. Scientists call these plants **conifers**. Cones are made up of overlapping scales. Seeds grow between the scales. As the seeds grow larger, the scales of the cone get thicker, darker, and harder.

As their seeds grow bigger, pinecones change from small and green to big and brown.

New conifers grow from the seeds released on the ground from other conifers.

Similar to fruits, cones help to transport seeds away from their parent plant. When conifer seeds are fully grown, the cone releases them. Some cones open their scales in dry weather and the seeds fall out. Other cones have scales that fall off, taking their seeds with them. Seeds start to grow into new conifers after falling to the ground.

WORD WISE

A CONIFER IS A TREE THAT HAS CONES AND SEEDS. THEIR LEAVES ARE NEEDLE-LIKE.

Seed Shapes and Sizes

Seeds are plant **embryos** that can grow into new plants after leaving the parent plant. Seeds come in all sorts of shapes and sizes. Some flowers make thousands of seeds so tiny you can hardly see them. A seed from a coconut tree is huge and can weigh around 4.5 pounds (2 kg). Every seed has what it needs to grow into a new plant already inside of it.

A seed is protected by its hard outer layer, called the seed coat. This layer protects the seed until it is ready to grow. Inside the seed are an embryo and food. The food nourishes the embryo until the seed can grow.

WORD WISE

AN EMBRYO IS THE BEGINNING STAGES OF A PLANT'S GROWTH INSIDE OF A SEED. EVENTUALLY, IT GROWS INTO A FULL-SIZED PLANT.

Seeds can be tasty! Many people enjoy snacking on sunflower seeds (pictured) or pumpkin seeds.

Roots and stems grow from a seed first. After, plant leaves begin to grow.

Spore Shapes and Sizes

Not every plant makes seeds. Some, such as ferns and mosses, make spores instead. Ferns and mosses release their spores, which then grow into new plants just like the parent plants.

Fern spores are very tiny. They are in packets under the fern's leaves. When the spores are ready to grow, they fall from the plant. Spores grow in damp places. They struggle to grow when it's hot and dry.

Fungi, such as mushrooms, reproduce with spores, too.

This illustration shows the life cycle of a moss.

Mosses are small, flowerless plants that grow on any surface with lots of water, such as damp rocks, fallen logs, and forest floors. Mosses grow stalks with packets of spores at the top. In dry weather, the packets open when the spores are ready to grow, and the spores soar away.

Consider This

Ferns and mosses produce millions of spores. Why is this a strong survival skill?

Buds and Bulbs

Some plants make bulbs that can grow into new plants. They grow underground. Bulbs are made up of layers of thick, overlapping leaves that grow around a **bud**. Inside the bud are the small parts needed for a new plant to grow.

There are bulbs we can eat! Some examples are onions (pictured), garlic, and chives.

Lilies (pictured), bearded irises, and tulips all grow from bulbs.

Bulbs help keep some plants alive during freezing winters. The leaves and other parts above ground die, but the bulb survives. In spring, the plant grows again from its bulb. Bulbs also can multiply. Small new bulbs grow from the side of the main bulb. Their buds separate from the parent plant when they're ready and grow into a new plant.

WORD WISE

A BUD IS A SMALL GROWTH ON A PLANT THAT BLOSSOMS INTO A NEW LEAF, FLOWER, OR SHOOT.

The Right Conditions

The right conditions are needed for a plant to grow successfully. When there is too little water, a plant wilts, or droops, and may die. When leaves don't get enough light, they can't make food, so the plant can't grow properly. Some plants die in areas that get a lot of sunshine because they need more shade.

Every part of a plant plays an important role to keep itself alive. Roots provide plants with water and hold them in the ground. Leaves make food for the plant. Flowers, fruits, and cones make seeds to grow new plants. With the right conditions—like enough water, nutrients, and light—the various plant parts work together to make a healthy plant.

Consider This

What is one similarity every plant has?
What's a difference you noticed between two different kinds?

Plants die if they don't get enough water, and they will also die if they receive too much water.

Glossary

attract To draw someone or something towards you.

coconut The large, oval, brown seed of a tropical palm.

concentration The amount of substance in a space.

environment A living thing's habitat, surrounded by other living things.

fern A leafy green plant that grows in shady spots.

iris A plant with long, pointed leaves and bright flowers.

nutrient The food that plants and animals need to grow and keep healthy.

overlapping Having parts that slightly cover each other.

parent plant The plant from which the seed of a new plant comes.

release To let go of something.

resource A physical material that living things need, such as air, water, and food.

soybean A seed in the legume family, which is a type of plant.

species A group of organisms with similar characteristics that can reproduce together.

spore The reproductive part of some plants, such as ferns and mosses.

sunflower A tall plant of the daisy family with large, golden flowers.

tree ring The layer of wood that grows on a tree's trunk each year.

For More Information

Books

Batchelor, Jacob. *Flowers, Leaves, and Other Plant Parts.* New York, NY: Children's Press, 2020.

Earley, Christina. *Plants.* Coral Springs, FL: Seahorse Publishing, 2023.

Hickman, Pamela. *Plants.* Toronto, ON: Kids Can Press, 2020.

Websites

National Geographic: Flowering Plants
www.natgeokids.com/uk/discover/science/nature/the-life-cycle-of-flowering-plants/#:~:text=Once%20the%20pollen%20grain%20lands,gametes%20in%20the%20'ovules
Find out more about the incredible role flowers play.

National Geographic: Plant and Animal Reproduction
education.nationalgeographic.org/resource/plant-and-animal-reproduction/
Explore the ways that plants and animals pass on their genes.

PBS LearningMedia: Plant Structure
thinktv.pbslearningmedia.org/resource/5dea21b4-6c92-46ff-982c-8650f9429c01/think-garden-plant-structure/
Learn about roots, stems, leaves, flowers, seeds, and fruit through engaging illustrations and animations.

Index